Prologue and a Warning

This is an honest, open book about what it takes to become a professional, self – employed artist in today's economic and social climate. I don't take any prisoners, pull any punches, or sugar coat anything in the coming pages. Will it bring out some haters, maybe make me some enemies? Sure, maybe, but it's not like it'll be the first time. I've done lots of things in my life that have made me enemies, so I don't much care anymore. Don't say I didn't warn you, if you choose to read beyond this point, you do so at your own risk. If you can't handle the realities of being a self – employed artist, put this book down now and call your boss and beg for your job back.

Being a successful artist is no easy task and the life isn't easy, but if you truly hear the call to express yourself artistically, and put in the years and years of hard work, you CAN see success, and yes, even money, good money.

You're about to embark on a remarkably interesting, raw, varied, and complex journey. It will be filled with highs and lows, triumphs, and frustrations. There will be days when you want to give up and others when you're so filled with passion that you can't sleep for the excitement. It's a long road to success, and it will be harder than anything you've ever done in your life, but it will also be the most rewarding and worthwhile.

Much of the advice I give in this book will be demonstrated through anecdotes, true stories from my own life and experiences over the past forty – odd years from class clown to internationally collected artist. You'll learn from the mistakes I made and the weird and wonderful things I picked up along the way. Some names have been changed to protect the guilty and innocent alike. Now, if you're ready, if you dare, take my hand down this darkened, twisted road, it might just lead to some light.

Carl B. Parker

Chapter 1: Who Is This "Parker" Guy & Why Should I Take His Advice?

Your first question is likely exactly what I've called this first chapter. Seriously, who is this guy to tell me about becoming a successful artist? Maybe you have a Masters degree in Fine Arts from some fancy pants university, or maybe you're a work a day person with some talent and a vague dream of walking away from your job in favour of a life filled with paint and freedom. Heck, maybe you don't even know whether you have any talent at all, maybe you just have a feeling in your soul that keeps pulling you toward art. Whoever you are, you have the same question if you've read this far, and I'll answer it for you.

The answer is in my memoirs, *Buy This Damn Book: Memoir of an Aspie Artist;* but seeing as you haven't bought "the damn book" yet (get it?), I'll briefly tell you who I am and how I have the audacity to tell you how to become a successful artist

I'm a kid from a broken home. I've suffered abuse, neglect, and loneliness. I've been ostracized, marginalized, and generally treated like crap. And I'm Autistic to boot (although that little bomb wasn't dropped on me until my mid 30's). I'm a high school drop out, and I've quit or been fired from more jobs than any human would rightly admit to. Seriously, I think I've had almost every entry level job known to human kind, shop keep, security guard, infantry soldier, labourer, food service, porter, call center agent; if there was a crap job, I had it and lost it.

I was, as you can see, a bit of a no – hoper. But through it all, I had my drawing pens, and eventually, my paint brushes. I taught myself to paint. I spent countless hours online and in libraries studying the old masters, all for free, because free was the only price I could afford. I worked my guts out! I mean that literally, I really did, sometimes going without sleep, fresh air and even food.

Now, I sell paintings all over the world; not through a gallery, not through any ecommerce site managed by a faceless corporation based in God Knows Where, and not through art fairs that charge exorbitant entry fees, but just on good old social media and other free or next to free platforms. One hundred percent of the proceeds go to me and me alone, no commissions or listing fees to pay. I've sold hundreds of paintings this way and I'm well on my way to becoming a household name. Some people may argue that I already am. So that's who I am to give you advice.

I'm also the guy who, by no exaggeration, probably made every career mistake that could ever be made. I've likely pulled myself from the ledge of career suicide more times than I even realize and it's these mistakes that you'll likely learn the most from.

That, and some of them are, in hindsight, pretty damn funny.

Chapter 2: Getting Started, A Note on Art

School: Who Needs It?

We've grown up in a society in which a proper education is seen as a necessary precondition to a profession. Nurses go to nursing school, teachers go to teachers' college, doctors go to medical school and lawyers go to law school. Thus, it stands to reason that the place those aspiring to be artists go is art school. I dispute this reasoning. Sure, there are people who will want to go, and if they have the time and tens of thousands of dollars and are into that sort of thing, they can fill their boots. But art school is not a necessary precondition to becoming a professional artist. It's utility in that regard is limited at best, and a detriment at its worst.

There are things art school can do and do well. It can teach you about art history, about various techniques and mediums and about creating in a studio environment. It can offer you the opportunity to try out other forms of art, such as sculpture or printmaking, or craft such as ceramics or textile work. It can be a place to meet great new friends who share your passion and love for the arts. And it can teach you all the lingo so you can talk the talk, so to speak.

Of course, it's not the "can dos" that lead me to the conclusion that art school is completely unnecessary to becoming an artist. It's more in the "can't dos" and "don't dos".

First, it can't give you the ability to create if you don't have it. You can study till the cows come home, but if you haven't got the talent, art school isn't going to give it to you. Putting lipstick on a pig doesn't change the fact that the pig is still a pig. In fact, many very well - regarded art schools don't even bother requiring prospective students to submit a portfolio. Let that sink in. The very institutions that claim to create artists don't bother to assess whether their incoming students have ever picked up a drawing pen or a paint brush or if they can draw a straight line. Maybe it's just me, but I would think a "small" thing like a modicum of talent might be a relevant consideration. Perhaps they're interested in something other than art, like, money.

Along the same line, art school can't give you passion for your work and the creative process. You have to have that already. It's something that comes from within your own heart and soul (although, on that note, it takes just one overly rigid or bitter instructor at one of these institutions to destroy your creative passion forever).

And now for the "don't dos". After reviewing several art school catalogue offerings over the years, I was absolutely astonished to learn that course offerings on the business end of art are glaringly absent, as are courses on sales or marketing. Odd considering the whole idea of becoming a professional artist is to be able to create art as a profession, i.e., to be able to make money by selling art. Art school won't teach you how to market your work, aside from maybe how to prepare the traditional portfolio (not terribly useful in today's increasingly online world). It doesn't bother to give a passing mention to how a prospective artist might price their work or set up an online gallery and website. It doesn't provide a class on record keeping and basic bookkeeping for the professional artist (the nasty Tax Man is going to have a field day with some of these graduates someday).

So, for tens of thousands of dollars over several years, art school can give you some art history, instruction on techniques and media, and allow you to play around with other forms of creativity. It can maybe help you make friends. Those are all things that, with a little discipline and a little creativity, you can get on your own for little or no money at all. You can study art history and the old masters, techniques, mediums and all that the same way I did, through self – directed study at the local library. You can check out books for free and learn to your heart's content. And if you don't feel like trapsing across town to go to the library, there's the wonderful world of the internet, just bursting with knowledge for you to consume, from museum and historical websites to free, yes free, online university classes.

If you want to try other forms of expression, you can just go try them. You don't need a professor to show you. And as for making friends with similar interests, well, join an arts co-op or an artist run centre for free or a nominal operating fee. Not only will you meet like minded people, but you might even get to show some of your work in the bargain.

In short, aside from the "college experience," art school can't give you anything that you can't get on your own. And it won't give you anything that will be useful to you and your art in any practical sense, not how to create your work, not how to tune into your deepest emotions and bring that to the canvas, and certainly not how or where to try to sell it when it's done. If that sounds like your cup of tea, go ahead, and enjoy, it's your time and money, but it's certainly not going to make an artist out of you.

Chapter 3: Talent and Hard Work, If You Don't Have Them, Keep the Day Job

You've probably heard the saying there's no such thing as an overnight success, right? Well, it's completely, one hundred percent true. I know, I know, I can hear you saying, "but hey, Mr. Painter Man, I read about a girl who painted such and such and she went viral and became filthy rich."

I guess I gave you more credit than I should have. Do you believe everything you read? Headlines about instant success are everywhere because headlines are about selling newspapers and getting readers. Who's going to read a story entitled, "Artist Makes Living After

Twenty Years of Hard Work"? I would, but that's me, and that's because I know the truth. Behind every so-called instant success story, there are two things, talent, and hard work and without both, you won't make a living as a professional artist.

Let's talk about talent first. What is it? I touched on it briefly in the previous chapter, but now it's time to take a deep dive into the concept. We all have a sense of what it is, but do we really know? In its simplest terms, talent is a natural aptitude or skill for something. We all know people who are talented in different areas, some can sing like angels, some can write tear – jerking poetry, some can run like the wind and others can handle a football like nobody's business. Others, like me, and I'm guessing, you, can draw or paint. We all know what it is, and we all know it when we see it.

But here's the thing, and it will likely offend some, but so be it. The truth is the truth. Talent is one of those things that you either have or you don't. It's just that simple. I can't tell you where it comes from, your grandmother, an accident of genetics, the way your brain is wired, some supernatural phenomenon, I have no idea, all I know is it's either there or it isn't.

You can prance around town all day brooding with a Salvador Dali moustache and a beat up old leather satchel telling people you're an artist, but if you have no talent, if you can't, for our purposes, paint or draw, you're just not. Go find what you're good at and do that.

Let's be brutally honest, we're all adults here. We know whether we have talent for something or not. We're not idiots. We know the difference between our mommies putting our pitiful drawings on the refrigerator when we were little to make us feel special and having an actual natural ability to do something and to do it better than most. Without that ability, you won't become a professional artist. Maybe you can paint or draw for fun, and if it makes you happy, that's fine, but without talent, you won't earn a dime. Art buyers are a surprisingly sophisticated bunch, and they know the difference between something by someone with a special ability to create and something thrown together by a poser.

Now, don't get me wrong, that doesn't mean people won't try. I've seen countless talentless hacks call themselves artists, post their work and try to sell it. With the advent of the internet, it seems like every other person you meet calls themselves an artist. It's become the default position for every unemployed Joe who refuses to go out and find something constructive to do and it's one of my biggest pet peeves!

Now that we have talent out of the way, let's talk about hard work. As with anything else, talent alone is a necessary, but not sufficient condition. You need to do something with it, exercise it, hone it, train it. That's where the hard work comes in. And that hard work will never end, as long as you want to make any money from your art. It may become different work, but the work never stops.

In the beginning, you'll want to work on your craft, your painting. Draw, and draw and when your hand gets sore, take a break, and then pick the pen back up and draw some more. The ability to draw is absolutely invaluable to being able to paint. Not only will it help you to sketch out your visions, but it also helps you with things like hand – eye coordination, line, control, perspective, etc. It's a foundational skill, like walking is to running, or learning the alphabet is to reading. Some people will disagree with this, postulating that drawing isn't essential to painting. To them I say the following, "everyone here who has sold literally hundreds of paintings from Atlanta to Australia

and Vancouver to Venice, raise their hand
…wait, what, only me? Well then, I rest my
case."

And of course, paint, paint whenever
you can. Experiment with different styles, learn
how your hands, eyes and mind come together in
the most natural way for you. Learn about art
history, about the great masters, look at their
work, read about them. Learn about techniques,
about shading and line and colour blending and
anything and everything else. Become a sponge
and soak it all up! I mentioned this before, but it
bears repeating, all this knowledge is readily and
easily available for free! Yes, that's right, free!
You don't need to go to art school, or to Fancy
Pants University, you can go online, you can go

to your local library, it's all there for the taking, so take it!

Over time, you'll begin to develop your own style. You'll become more confident in your expression and the results. You'll fall in love with not only the act of painting, but with the paintings you've created. You'll begin to show others, family, friends. You'll be excited to start selling, and to that I say, hang on just a cotton-picking minute, your work isn't done. In fact, it's just started!

Sure, maybe your Auntie or your best friend from grade 4 might hand you some cash for one of your masterpieces, but that's not the same as earning an actual living as an artist. You won't eat for long if you think friends and relatives are going to continually open their wallets to you. It just doesn't work that way. They may love your work, but they have bills too, and let's be honest, how many paintings does Aunt Gertie really have room for?

So, you'll need to get the public interested in your work. You know, all those people out there, millions of them, eager to spend their hard-earned money on stuff and some of that stuff might be art, maybe even your art. And that's where the hard work comes in.

For the public to buy your art, they have to know about you. Not only do they have to know about you, they must like you and trust you. There are no shortcuts here, you will, if you genuinely want to make a living as a professional artist, work long and hard to establish and maintain a presence and a reputation. No sane person is going to hand over their hard-earned money to some fly – by – night person claiming to be an artist they've never heard of.

With all that in mind, ask yourself, assuming you have the talent, are you ready and willing to do the work? Are you ready to put years into it? Long, tough years. Years in which you may lose family or friends, where people will think you've completely lost your mind. Years of wonderful highs and crushing lows. If the answer is yes, welcome to the club, you're ready for chapter 4.

Chapter 4: You've Thought About It, Think Again!

I know, I know, you already thought about it and you're all in. You're fired up and ready to rumble. It won't be that hard, right? They always say when you do what you love, it's not like work at all. Well, I don't know who "they" are, but I can tell you they are wrong! So, I'm going to ask you to think again, and think hard, harder than you've ever thought about anything.

Take some time for yourself, by yourself. Go camping, go fishing or something, by yourself. If you can't get away, find some time when you can sit alone, quietly with just good old "me, myself and I." No wife, no husband, no kids, no friends, no family, no other people, just you. I'll let you have your cat with you if you must. Now, just think about your life, how it is now, your job, if you have one, your family, if you have one. Think about your art, and about what you genuinely want. Take that romantic picture of being celebrated by the champagne swilling elite as you unveil your latest offering in New York while you pose for the paparazzi right out of your head. While you're at it, take the mansion, the fancy jet – setting lifestyle and the million dollar price tag attached to your paintings out of your head too, along with the family and friends bowing at your feet and showering you with praise. That's all fantasy, and while fantasy is fun, I don't peddle such nonsense. I offer reality and while it won't always be pretty, it will always be the truth.

Can you handle going to your wife, husband, significant other, parents, whoever, and telling them you've decided to put all you've got into making this art thing work? Can you handle telling them you're quitting your job or cutting your hours, or simply devoting the vast majority of your free time in this endeavor? Can you handle the confused looks on their faces, the protests, the opposition, the suggestion that you might just have gone mad? Maybe none of that will happen. Maybe you'll be more fortunate than I was Maybe you have supportive people around you. Then again, maybe not. People, in my experience, do not react well to change, particularly when that change involves good old-fashioned dollars and cents and what they perceive as some ethereal notion of "being an artist". Are you ready for that? Are you ready to talk about it, to argue about it, to stand firm in the face of opposition, to show them what you're planning and how you'll go about it? If all this makes you queasy, you're not ready, come back later. But if you've given it due consideration and you're ready for the hard conversations, you're on your way.

Once you get yourself comfortable with the conversations you'll have to have, you'll need to come to terms with how hard and how much work this journey will involve and what it may cost you. You're about to work harder and longer than you ever had, often without any tangible reward, and you'll do it for years!

You'll start selling paintings for small sums, $75 or $100 and some weeks you'll sell a couple, and then you'll go weeks or months without even a sniff. And even getting to that point might take years. Know that and learn to manage your funds accordingly.

You'll have small victories and huge defeats. You'll learn more than you ever have. You'll experience euphoric joys and the depths of despair. You'll have days when you want to throw all your paints away and become a monk and other days when you can't bear to put them away because the flow is so great. And through it all, you'll lose people, friends, lovers, maybe some family. Some won't understand what you're doing. Some will resent the time you once devoted to them being spent on your art career. Some will just be simple nay-sayers who feel the need to stick their negative beak in at every opportunity, reminding you of the thousands of artists that never make a dime and the harsh realities of your impractical, irresponsible choice.

If I had a dollar for every person I lost along the way, I'd hardly have to paint any more. But it's like this, at least in my life, you're either for me or you're against me and if you fall into the latter camp, see yourself out. Most will go on their own, but some might need a gentle nudge.

So, if you've tossed this all around your noggin and you're still absolutely certain this is what you want to do, you're ready to get into the meat of it.

Chapter 5: Keep It In Your Pants!

Now that I have your attention, calm down, I'm not talking about sex, that will come later, I promise, I'm talking about your wallet. You've done a lot of work, you've honed your talent, you're ready to get out there and make this art thing a going concern, but now what? Where do you turn? If you're anything like I was in the beginning, you turn to galleries. I mean, that's the image you have, right, you paint them, and a gallery sells them for you for a small fee, easy peasy, lemon squeezy.

Obviously, you haven't grasped the theme of this book. There is no easy peasy. And as for galleries, I have my own opinions and they will come in a later chapter. Suffice to say, I manage to make a living without the aid of a gallery, and I get to keep one hundred percent of my proceeds, not half, but that's a story for later.

Back to what we were talking about, your pants, and the wallet that's in them. This is an online world and when you start looking around for places to showcase your art and galleries that might be interested in representing you, you'll do what we all do, you'll google it. And you'll find a staggering number of galleries, both brick and mortar and online, all with very impressive looking sites. Some will show very impressive photos of the "art set", sipping that champagne I told you to forget about while admiring the work of some beautiful young new artist. They're very eager to accept submissions and say so right up front, on every page of their site. They are committed to discovering and nurturing emerging artists, that's the line. Of course, to add credibility, they talk about a vetting process with their curators and they're invariably based in Chelsea or West End London.

The application process is always simple, plug a few simple details into the online form provided and a few pictures of your work and there you go, you've made your first submission to a gallery. Heck, sometimes, they'll even find your details and come to you.

You'll feel a rush of euphoria; you've done it, you've put yourself out there, your work, your guts, your passion. And you'll wait, weeks, months, days, who knows, until you open your email one day and you've been accepted! You're good enough, your work has been accepted by a fancy gallery, in a major world art centre! You can hardly feel your feet as you walk on air! It's everything you dreamed of and it wasn't even that hard, clearly that Parker guy was full of it! You're in like Flynn, there's just the small matter of the fee. You know, a nominal fee for things like printing promotional materials, online presence, hosting events. I mean what's a couple thousand dollars when you've been "discovered"?

I'll tell you what it is, it's pure and utter crap! I know, I know, all you want to hear right now is how good your work is, how you're the next big thing. You've worked so hard; maybe you've lost your wife or husband. You've gone countless nights without sleep; you've let yourself get fat, or far too thin, it's your damn turn, I get it. The thing is, it's not. I very nearly fell into this trap, but I was fortunate enough to have a wife that is one shrewd cookie.

Let me break it down for you. Traditional art galleries take a large commission from art sales, somewhere from 40 to 60%. They do that to cover their expenses, the building, staff, events, promotion, that sort of thing. They don't ask you for money up front. And if they did get a couple grand up front, what incentive would they have to actually sell your work? Think about it, if you're getting say 10 artists to pay you $2,000 just as a fee for allegedly representing you, why would they bother to market your work? They have your money already. These tricksters are called vanity galleries. They prey on the hopes and dreams of artists, take your cash and give very little, if anything, in return. Bottom line, if a gallery wants you to give them money up front for representation, run, run like hell and run fast!

Sadly, preying on the hopes and dreams of artists has become big business and vanity galleries aren't the only culprits. Email scammers will come along with various tales about their wives or whatever seeing your website and wanting several pieces. Every artist's dream, right, to sell 5 or 6 pieces at once? But there's a catch, he can only pay by credit card and you have to use his shipping company. Again, run. I considered going along with one of these, I figured, why not, take the money and so what if it's a scam or a fake credit card number, it's not my problem. But it is, once the scam is revealed, your bank will yank that money right away from you as fast as you can say scam. Then, you've lost your money, several of your best paintings and you may just end up finding a police officer at your door because you've landed smack in the middle of a money laundering operation.

Then, of course, there are the contests and calls for submission that want a fee. A fee just for submitting your work. I'm sorry, you want $40 to just look at my work? Let me say it again, they want YOU to pay THEM to look at your work and to judge whether it's worthy of being included in their show. Again, where is the incentive to sell anything at this alleged show? I'll take it one step further, what's the incentive to even have a show? They've gotten $40 from, let's say 1000 artists desperate to show their work somewhere, anywhere. Why bother paying venue fees, promotional fees, any fees at all? Just fold up the tent, take down the website and take off with everyone's loot! They have your money already, along with hundreds like you. I know, it's only $40, but those bills add up and if you look hard enough, you can find legitimate places to submit your work for free.

I will make a small note here about artist run centres. Sometimes they will charge a nominal fee for hanging, once they've accepted you for a show, like $20 or so, and that's legit. They're small outfits that rely on ever dwindling government funding for their existence, run by volunteers and they're generally very upfront about the fact.

There are more variations on scams targeting artists than I can even count. It's become a huge industry for many unscrupulous people. I have some very simple advice for you, first, if it sounds too good to be true, it is. Second, and please, I can't stress this enough, if you have to pay to play; if you have to give money up front for representation, to be included in a book or magazine, or to even have a shot at being accepted for a show, move on. Keep your wallet in your pants, you're here to learn how you can make a living for yourself,

not for someone else.

Chapter 6: A Small Note on Outsider Art Sites

My opinion on outsider art and outsider art websites isn't going to win me any friends, I know that. I also don't care, I'm not Dale Carnegie and I don't care about "winning friends and influencing people," at least insofar as it requires me to lie to them.

If you're not familiar with the term "outsider art," it refers to art which supposedly lay outside the mainstream art world. It goes by a variety of names, including the ridiculously pretentious "art brut" and those who profess to be outsider artists are generally self – taught. Thing is, most of them had really bad teachers and it shows! Does that sound harsh? Well, as the kids say these days, sorry, not sorry. Because it's true. I know, I know, these outsider artists call their style naïve. You know what that means? It's a fancy way of saying they draw or paint like a six-year-old. That's fine if you are, in fact, a six–year-old. Put your artwork on the fridge for the family to see and leave the fine art to the big kids.

"Come on, Carl," I can hear you saying, "what's the harm? I mean it gives people who wouldn't have a chance to show their work someplace to do just that." Well the harm is that it's basically lying to people and giving them some sort of illusion of having any hope at being a professional artist. Let me explain.

When you go to one of these sites, the first thing you'll see is a definition of outsider art and it will be pretty much as I just described. Here's the thing, they claim to be outside the "mainstream art world". What on earth is the mainstream art world? There isn't one, not one that matters anyway. Traditional galleries are rapidly disappearing and losing their stranglehold on the art scene as operational costs continue to skyrocket and as more and more art collection is done via the internet. There is no club that these so-called outsider artists are being kept out of.

Granted, some of them may have been rejected from various traditional galleries and this frustration is exactly what these sites feast upon. They very cleverly rebrand the source of that frustration, the fact that the art itself simply isn't worthy of consideration, into something revolutionary, anti-establishment, and part of the counterculture. All of a sudden, that artist feels better because they aren't a talentless hack, they're, to take a very old phrase, sticking it to the man, they're rebels with a brush. And they get that all, you guessed it, for a nominal fee. In my case, it wasn't cash that exchanged virtual hands, it was a painting. Everyone who wished to be featured on a particular outsider art website was required to send the owner of said site a painting, free and once received, you could be on the site. Oh, and I was promptly removed from the site as quickly as I was added.

You still may think that all sounds harmless. Let the baby have the bottle and all that, but really, it's not. Aside from a tiny number of artists involved in this outsider scene, they really do lack any artistic talent whatsoever. Giving people false hope about their prospects and lying to them about their talent or lack thereof serves no purpose at all. It's nothing but false flattery to achieve some sort of gain. It's like the dress shop salesclerk who works on commission and tells you how fabulous you look in that bright orange taffeta monstrosity that costs $2000. You'll walk out looking like a fat, shiny pumpkin, but she's going to get paid!

Chapter 7: A Note About Traditional Galleries

Traditional galleries, to be represented by one is pretty much every emerging artist's dream, at least starting out. It was mine too. I courted many galleries, sending out submissions, waiting eagerly to be judged worthy to join the ranks of those already allowed "in" as it were. I even did business with a few. I mean that's where it all happens, right? The shows, the sales, the champagne. They're the experts in selling art, why wouldn't any artist with half a brain want to get into one?

Well, I'm not an artist with half a brain, I actually have a whole, fully functioning one and although I'm sure there are several fine, reputable galleries out there, I am not interested in dealing with them. Maybe you are but follow my logic here for a bit.

First and foremost, and really this is a new argument against the traditional brick and mortar gallery, but they are seriously "so 2010!" With social distancing, mask mandates and limits on gatherings, these spaces are quickly becoming things of the past. I mean, who wants to get all dressed up in their finery, to stand in line to be allowed into an art opening held in some small room or series of rooms? Does the mask have to match the shoes? Yawn and yuck!

Further, let's be brutally honest here, even before this Covid stuff, galleries were quickly moving toward extinction. Let's face it, art is a tough business and commercial rents are high. With the online world being what it is, an easy, open marketplace for anything and everything one could ever want, all traditional retail outlets are having a hard time. Imagine selling a luxury, non-essential item like art. Yeah, galleries are dying and dying fast.

Still not convinced? Okay, let me come at this in a more direct and personal way; let's talk cash. Traditional galleries, the reputable ones, sell on commission. They accept your work on the basis that if a work sells, they get anywhere from 40 to 60% off the top. You read that right, 40 to 60%. To make the math easy, we'll use a 50% commission. For every $500 painting you sell through Gallery X, you'll get $250.

If that's not bad enough, there's more.

Galleries are sophisticated business. You'll

have to sign an agreement allowing them

exclusivity within a certain territory, it could be

the state, the country, wherever. But what it

means is you can't sell your work within that

territory any other way, through any other means

except through them. So, if your sister's best

friend's brother wants to buy one of your

paintings for a wedding gift for his buddy, you

have to send him to the gallery, you have no

freedom to negotiate a price or to sell it to him

directly, you're stuck with the gallery and your

half and that's it.

Does it still sound like a good deal?

Maybe it does, I mean they are doing the work,

right? They're out there constantly promoting

your work. They're spending their days working for you, doing the jobs you don't want to do, right? But are they? Are they really?

No, no they aren't. And here's why. Go to pretty much any decent gallery website and click on their list of artists. Now, count them. There are dozens, if not well over a hundred. Simple logic tells a person that no gallery can provide equal, let alone adequate attention to that many artists. Someone's work is ending up in storage, at least for some while. And while that work, maybe your work, is sitting in the gallery basement, your hands are tied. Seven people could contact you dying to buy it, and all you can do is say, call Gallery X.

Do you really want to get lost in the crowd? I'm assuming not because, if you've read this far, it's pretty clear you believe you have something special to offer. Do you really want your hands tied? Do you really want someone dictating to whom and under what circumstances and at what price you can sell your work, you know the work you've poured your heart and guts into? And do you really want to give over half of your money for the so-called privilege?

If you've answered "no", then you might be ready to go it alone. It's not for the faint of heart. I told you before, it'll be hard, hard work, but it can be done, and the best part is, when it works out, you get to keep your money!

Chapter 8: Alternatives to The Brick and Mortar

Gallery in the Real World

You're probably asking where you're

supposed to show your art if you're not in a

gallery or not paying out fees to be considered

for shows. Well, in the pre-Covid world, and

when things finally get back to normal, all kinds

of places. The next time you're out and about in

your local community, take a good look around

at your surroundings.

Did you stop for lunch or a coffee?

What did you notice on the walls of the coffee

shop or restaurant? Anything? Pictures,

maybe? Perhaps even paintings? Many bistros,

restaurants, cafes, etc. are more than happy to

showcase the works of local artists on their walls. First, it saves them buying art outright. Second, it fosters the good will of the community for the business; it just looks good to support the local art scene. Finally, and most importantly for you, it gets your work right in front of the eyeballs of dozens, maybe hundreds of people every week.

Next time you notice art hanging in a local eatery, ask your server or the manager where they get their art. They'll gladly tell you. Approach the manager or owner, at a time convenient to them, and certainly not during busy times (don't expect to be taken seriously if you try to bring up your art during a lunch or dinner rush), and explore the possibility of showcasing your work there for a period of time, generally anywhere from 1 to 3 months. Be prepared to show some pictures of your work. Avoid showing any work that contains nudity or controversial or disturbing imagery, eating establishments are open to all members of the public, young and old, sensitive, and not, it's not the place for your political statements on canvas.

If the owner or manager is receptive, discuss terms upfront. Some owners will provide you the wall space for free, others may ask for a small commission (usually around 10%) for any work that sells from their space. I've had both arrangements, and while I, of course prefer not having to share my proceeds, 10% is an entirely reasonable amount for a business owner to ask.

Then, you arrange a time to go over and hang your work. This again must be done at the convenience of the business and likely during a time when it isn't open to the public. Come prepared with the proper tools and of course, your work. In some cases, there will already be nails there for you to simply place your work on, other work having been removed. In other cases, there won't be. Always, always ask before you start hammering into the walls of the business. And of course, measure, check, and double check before you do so that you get the hanging right the first time.

Make sure you have little cards made up, business card size, with the name of the painting, the size, your name, contact information and price printed on them for each piece. Ideally, you'll have done these on your computer and printed them, but if you must print, do it very neatly. If you can't be neat, get someone to do it for you. If your information card is messy, it's unprofessional at best, and at worst, even if someone does want to contact you to purchase a piece they've seen, they won't be able to because the card is illegible.

In the earlier years of my career, I showed in various eating establishments with varying degrees of success. Sometimes my work sold like gangbusters. For example, in one café, I sold 6 paintings within a little over a month. Other times, I may have sold a couple. In any event, it does get your work out there in front of the public and it can draw traffic to your website (yes, you need one, and I'll discuss that in a later chapter).

Another place you may wish to check out is your local gift shop. Sometimes, they'll let you place a piece in their window, or even offer one for sale in the shop. Keep in mind, they are likely going to expect a commission of 30 or 40%. That being said, they won't likely have a stable of artists they stock and will be more likely to actively show customers your pieces, eager to sell such a high value item to the browsing tourist.

And don't overlook your good old local library. You won't be able to place pieces there for outright sale, exactly, but often libraries are open to showcasing the work of local artists in their windows or on their walls, as an exhibit or a feature. The benefit for you is your name and work will be in front of all the library patrons, and some may contact you about a piece they've seen and wish to purchase after the exhibit is over. Also, because a library is a reputable, respected public place, you can add the showing to your artist C.V. as an exhibition.

Along the same line as the library, but even better, are government buildings. Often, state, provincial, local, and even national governments will put out public calls for submission for artworks to hang in their various buildings for a certain period of time. These submissions are always at no cost to the artist and if your art is accepted, it will hang in a designated government space, being seen by, government ministers, business leaders and visiting dignitaries alike. It's a tremendous honour and again, a great thing to have on a C.V. Let's face it, it's straight up bragging rights and it sounds quite impressive.

I have had, and currently have a piece hanging in our provincial legislature's dining room. Every day, the premier, departmental ministers, staff, visiting people of considerable import, as well as tourists, see my work while they chow down. In short, the most important people in the province, as well as sometimes the most important people in the country, look at MY painting (along with those of other artists) while they dine. There's no way that's a bad thing. In fact, it's pretty damn cool.

So, get out there, open your eyes to the possibilities all around you. Don't be shy, talk to people, ask questions, the worst they can say is no, and you never know, they might say yes.

Chapter 9: The Power of Social Media

When you're first starting out, you'll likely be looking for low cost, or free ways to showcase your art, unless of course you have tons of money to burn. I didn't and don't, so I started out posting my work on various social media sites I was already using anyway. In fact, social media is still the way a vast majority of my work sells.

People are visual creatures, they like to look at pretty things, let those pretty things be your work.

Sites like Facebook are invaluable to an artist. Your friends and family will see your posts, as will their friends. Some will share your posts, thereby expanding their reach and suddenly, your paintings are in front of hundreds, if not thousands of eyes! Not bad considering all you did was post a few pictures.

Speaking of posting pictures, let me be clear, you are aiming to be a professional working artist which means your pictures have to look the part. Get a decent camera; it doesn't have to be expensive, a good digital point and shoot one will do just fine. Pay attention to the lighting, you want your work showcased in the best possible light, pardon the pun. It can't be too dark, and there can't be glare streaming across it. Full light or daylight is best if you can get it. It sounds really simple, doesn't it, I mean it's taking a freakin' picture, how hard can it be? Hard. I'm serious and I can't stress enough how important the picture is! The picture you post is what potential buyers and fans of yours will see. It's how they judge you and your work, make a good impression. It's so easy to get excited about your latest masterpiece. I know. I get it. You just completed this great work of art, you know in your guts it will sell and sell fast, and all you want is to slap that baby on social media and wait for the accolades and the eventual, "is this for sale?" What I'm trying to say, albeit gently is, if the picture you take is shit, the painting won't sell, so don't rush through this crucial first step.

I have seriously seen myself take over a dozen pictures of a given piece only to find none of them represented my work in a way that pleased me. Too light, too dark, glare, funny angle, I've had every problem known to humankind in that department, you just have to be patient.

Then, of course, there's the cropping. If you're doing just a picture of your painting, you'll want to crop out all the background stuff. This can easily be done on your computer with a photo editing program. Again, don't be hurried or sloppy, crop it properly.

And on the editing front, I suggest not fooling with filters or the colours. The goal is to have a picture of the painting as it actually looks. There's nothing that will alienate a buyer more than receiving a piece that she thought was one colour and finding out it was another. The devil really is in the details!

Now, back to patience for a moment, if you haven't gotten the message already, let me repeat it, sales are not going to come in over night. This is a process, a long one. Your goal here is to steadily develop a presence, a reputation. Post often, but don't spam, nobody likes a salesman. Thank people when they say nice things about your work, be gracious. Show some interest in others, their lives, what they post. Ask some of your friends if they mind you posting your work on their feeds so their friends can see it (always, always ask, never post on someone's feed without permission, it's just douchy.).

Get yourself on more than one social media site to expand your presence. Art is a numbers game and there are a lot of artists out there competing for attention and sales. That, and I once read somewhere that only about one percent of the population ever buys original art. If that statistic is true, you have about 5 potential buyers among your 500 Facebook friends.

In addition to social media, don't be afraid to post a free ad on a sale site, you know Kijiji, Craigslist, whatever site is popular where you live. You'd be surprised the things people will buy. A free add, at least on Kijiji, will allow you to post several pictures of your work, and you might just get a sale or two. When I first started, before I joined any social media site (I did so late and ironically enough, reluctantly), I posted my work on Kijiji and managed to get several sales from local art collectors, without spending a dime on promotion, just a few minutes of my time.

The truth is many people won't buy. In fact, the vast majority won't, but they may love your work. People have lives and bills and circumstances. Some people can't afford, or think they can't afford original art. There are ways around that, and I'll discuss that in a later chapter. However, don't write these people off, many of them will become your biggest ambassadors, and they work for free! They'll share your work, they'll sing your praises, and you just never know who they know. Maybe they have no money, but their boss might, or their sister or their friend from college who now lives way across the country and has a great job. Never count people out.

Eventually, if you keep at it, a message will appear, and it will be a sale! And one sale will turn into more as you become better known and liked. It's how I make my living, and I live quite well, if I do say so myself.

Chapter 10: Integrity, Artistic and the Normal Kind...Have It, Keep It, Practice It

Okay, kids, this, as you may have guessed is the don't be a jerk chapter. I can almost hear you saying, "does he really think we need to be told not to be jerks?" Yes, yes I do think that, both because I know what people are like and because I have been one many times myself.

Let's start with artistic integrity. Once you begin selling work, you will LOVE IT! You'll be on a high that no drug could ever give. You'll become almost addicted to the process, the painting, the posting, the selling, the money! You'll feel like some sort of art god or goddess!

Now, confidence and self esteem is great, but there's an arrogance that can creep in so subtly that you don't even notice it until it's too late.

It goes something like this, and I did it in my younger days. You've gone without a sale for, let's say ten days. You're feeling annoyed, you can't understand what the problem is with "these people on social media". You decide you'll paint something you know is sure to sell. You don't know it yet, but you've made your first mistake right there.

Your arrogant ass goes into the studio and whips up something that may or may not be reminiscent of a piece you did sell, not the same, but in the same vein. There's really no feeling in it, you just want a sale because you think you're due, and there's a sale on leather jackets that you can't bear to miss.

You finish it, you post it, and you wait. Crickets. Why? I'll tell you why, art collectors are a savvy bunch and your fans will be no different. They know the best work you produce, and they expect and want it and rightfully so. Sure, your half-assed painting might be better than what 99% of the population could ever produce, but do you want a half - assed effort from your surgeon, or mechanic, lawyer, or other professional? Of course not! Your collectors and your art deserve better. I'm lucky, I haven't done this in decades, mostly because I don't have to, but also because I know. When I paint a piece, I wait. I let it sit for a bit, maybe an hour, maybe a few, and then I go back and look. If I'm not sure, I know it's not done. Not every piece will be a masterpiece, it's just a fact, and that's okay as long as you learn the difference.

Now, for just plain old integrity, basically, you have to do what you say and say what you do. If you sell a painting, you have to ship it promptly, provide a tracking number so collectors know when it's arriving. Set prices that make sense and keep them consistent. Don't charge one price for one person because you need the sale and then charge someone you know has a bit of coin four times that amount for a painting of the same size just because you know he or she has it. Word gets around, people talk, and they talk faster and more furious about bad things than good. If there's a problem, work to correct it. Most people are decent and aren't out to scam you and it's easy to tell the ones that are.

Be gracious, a thank you costs you nothing at all. Be available, I don't mean allow all your time to be tied up, but if a collector just handed you a nice sum for a piece, be prepared to hear their story about why that particular piece spoke to them. Actually listen and respond, it's good for you and for them, they're sharing a bit of their life with you because something you did moved them. It's a wonderful, almost sacred exchange. Collectors want to talk to the artist, it's just the way it is. They want you to know why they love a given piece, they want to know your process, they want to feel heard and like you care beyond getting the cash. There are limits, of course, and again, that will be the subject of a later chapter, but most people just want to chat a bit about the piece they just bought with the genius that created it.

Speaking of collectors, you'll be very excited to post your works as sold on social media as they sell. It's a nice selling strategy, people see your work is being collected by others, which may make them feel more secure in taking the leap themselves. Never, never ever post the name of a collector without express permission! I cannot stress this enough. Never disclose the buyer, it's a transaction between you and them and it's not anyone else's business. If the buyer wants to brag, that's up to them, but you keep your big trap shut! What I do is just post the country, for example, "sold to a cool lady in the USA, or sold to a kick-ass dude in Australia". It gets the message across and it maintains the privacy of the collector.

Most of this is just common sense, be nice, be gracious, be engaging, be honest, avoid posting controversial or offensive content. In short, just don't be a jerk.

Chapter 11: Your Own Website, Yes, You Do
Need One.

Okay, now I'm going to tell you to open

your wallet. Don't panic, it won't cost you

much, maybe forty bucks. Heck, even I could

afford it, so I'm sure you can. It's time to get

yourself a proper website. Something that

showcases your work, something professional

looking, something you spend a little time on.

This website will be "mission control" as far as

your art business goes, and make no mistake,

you are running a business. That may sound

distasteful to you now. I can hear you saying,

"but I create for the love of it, don't sully it up

with talk of crass mercantilism." To that I say,

get over yourself, cupcake, whine about your distaste for the almighty dollar at your weekly Young Marxists' Club, you bought this book because you want to make a living from your art, that means you want people to give you money in exchange for your art. Money in exchange for a good or service is a business, so get your head around it now. It's not evil, it's not selling out. It's reality, you have a skill, you create beautiful things, and you need to eat, and have shelter and heat and a car or a bus pass.

With that digression out of the way, for now, there will be more on this later, let's get back to the website. You want to appear credible, successful, like you can afford at least the forty bucks for a website, so spring for the unique domain name if you possibly can. You know what I mean. Go to the web hosting site of your choice, there are tons of them, Weebly, Wix, Wordpress, Go Daddy, to name a few, pick whichever one works for you, and create a website. They're all pretty user friendly, even for a luddite such as myself. I was raised in a time when floppy disks were still a thing and DOS seemed cool, then I dropped out of school, and I still managed to create a decent website, so you can too. Pay the extra for the InsertNameHereArtist.com rather than the InsertArtistNameHere.webhostingservice.com. People will remember it more easily and as I said before, it will give you an air of credibility.

On the site, have a homepage, with the normal homepage things, a welcome, maybe a nice picture of you and maybe your current best piece. Then, have an "About the Artist" page. People love to read about other people's stories and struggles. Did you go to school? Did you have a particularly tough struggle you're willing to talk about? What inspires your work? That kind of stuff, along with the mundane, "born and raised" things.

And of course, you'll want a gallery page where you showcase your currently available work. Remember those awesome pictures you took for social media? Well, those will come in very handy here, post them, plug in the details, and voila, you have a gallery.

Just a note on the gallery, I don't care if you have 45 paintings for sale, post no more than 10, your 10 best, at a time. You can rotate

them, if you like, but no more than 10, ever!
Why? Are you really asking me why? Because,
if you post 45 paintings, it's obvious you haven't
sold a piece, probably ever. That or you're just
slapping paint around like some hack.
Remember, your aim is to be a professional
working artist, resist the urge to show it all, and
just give them your best 10.

The next page is optional, but for me, it
was the smartest decision that was ever made for
me. I say it that way because a trusted advisor
suggested it (more on surrounding yourself with
trusted advisors later). A blog. Yeah, I know,
you're an artist, not a writer. You don't have
time. The work is so good it sells itself. No, no,
and no. First, no one cares that you're an artist
and not a writer, if they've come to your

website, they already know that. I'm hoping I can safely assume you can string words together in some sort of coherent fashion. If not, find one of those trusted advisors to proofread for you. And as for time, make it. I promise it will be worth your while. People that buy art are looking for a personal connection to a piece. Sometimes, the connection is obvious, you painted a frog pond in spring and the collector happened to remember her childhood chasing frogs in a pond just like the one you painted. Sometimes it's not that instantaneous. Sometimes, actually more often than not, it's the mood, the emotion behind the piece, especially if your work is leaning more toward the abstract. People love a story, and if the image and the story resonate, you likely have a sale! Give them that story.

And, I'm sorry, hotshot, your work does not sell itself. My work doesn't even sell itself, per se. It takes work, hard work, and potential collectors want to know you, they want to know why you painted what you did, what you felt, what inspired you. Never discount the human element, you're a human and you're trying to get humans to spend their hard-earned money on something you created. Take the half hour, open yourself up and write the damn blog post. First, you'll want to do it fairly regularly, twice, three times a week, to get people used to it, then you may transition to writing a post only when you create a piece. Then post the blog all over social media for your fans to read. Don't be afraid to be a bit vulnerable if it's honest. Collectors, as I've said before, are more sophisticated than you think, they know garbage when you're peddling it. Some of the quickest sales I've had are when the magic on the canvas meets the true emotion I felt and expressed in my blog. I'll give you an example, I once painted a piece with a man in a boat in a swirling sunset that was inspired by my rekindling a relationship with a love I had lost more than once over the span of 30 years and hadn't seen for at least 20. We reconnected and called our love "the Vortex" because that's what it felt like, like we were literally "sucked in" with no choice. I wrote openly and honestly about it, and BAM, it sold, and for a tidy sum. People want to know you, share as much as you comfortably can. Oh, and allow people to comment on your posts. And respond, promptly and faithfully. People love to be engaged with what you're doing.

Finally, add a "Contact Me" form so people can contact you. The inquiries will go straight to your email.

Along the same line, I'm sure your next question is whether you should pay the extra for a shopping cart on your site. This is a tough one, so I'll tell you my experience and you can make up your own mind. The lure of the shopping cart is obvious. You go to bed at night and wake up to hundreds, if not thousands of dollars in sales. I've tried it at least 5 times, with no success whatsoever!

The website, I submit, is not a direct sales site, but it is, with the gallery, the blog, and all of that, a showcase for you and your work. You're regularly sharing the blog on social media. Don't pay the extra for shopping cart functionality. It's one of the biggest scams in history and you'll make nothing. People will want to talk to you, in my experience. They want to tell you what a piece means to them, they'll want to ask questions, they want to size you up.

This also gives you flexibility in pricing. If a past collector approaches you and wants a small deal, without the shopping cart, you have that flexibility. If a collector has purchased 3 paintings, I have no problem eating shipping on a 4th. Ya feel me? People want to feel safe, they want to hear from you, you the artist, personally, they want to know how much shipping is, they want you to know why they love the piece. They need to trust you. Art is a business of communication, and for me, that communication and flexibility is key. You're offering one-of-a-kind works, not run of the mill prints, don't treat your work as such. Showcase them professionally on your website and check your email regularly for inquiries.

Chapter 12: To Print or Not to Print, That Is the Question

There's no question, some artists make some decent coin from prints. There are all kinds of sites where you can sell prints of your work, and I've tried more than a few. It's a seemingly attractive option, post a pic of the work, and then just let the site do its work. Of course, thousands of people will buy your prints, right? I mean 4 or 5 people on Facebook have asked you if you sell prints.

Again, this is a mistake I had to make more than once. People routinely ask me about prints, and I've had to say no, like I said after trying it several times. I mean all the so-called advice websites say you totally should do it. Well, what I've learned about those advice websites is "those who can do, those who can't write advice websites."

If your work is truly good, truly original, if you really have a unique style, your collectors don't want you out there making prints for every moron with $13. They just don't. They've paid hundreds of dollars for a piece that touches them, it's in their home, they can smell the wood of the canvas bars, they can feel the texture of the paint. It's an experience that stays with them forever, the emotional connection, the sensory experience. Why would you cheapen that with an 8x10" on glossy paper?

This is where some of that integrity comes into play. I know, you have rent due and you're out of bananas and milk, but this is a long game. You're establishing a reputation, a collectability, a rarity of your work. Someone that's paid $300 for an original doesn't want to visit someone who paid $12.99 for a print.

I'll be honest, I've tried every variation of this, from the standard print on demand sites, to contracting a custom printer and not only does the math not work out, but you're spitting in the faces of the people who have bought your originals.

Here's an example from my country, Canada. Here, everyone has heard of Catherine Karnes Munn, she was a pretty big deal. I think she might actually still be alive, but her framed prints are selling on social media and Kijiji for $15 and $20. In economics, there's such a thing as saturation of the market. I'm sure she's a nice lady, but the public is, frankly, exhausted with her and it shows in the print prices. On a graph in economics, supply and demand intersect at a point where things sell….in her case, think about it. People are offering her prints for the price of a case of beer. No comment on her talent, but I think the business acumen speaks for itself.

You want to create something sustainable. You want to create a legacy, a rarity. Shout the fact you don't do prints loud and proud. Your collectors will thank you. I hate to say it, but no one wants to go to their secretary's house and see a print of their original. Figure out what kind of artist you want to be. Do you want to honour those people who spent good money on your original work, or do you want to be a sad sellout with no money and no legacy?

Chapter 13: Art Is A Business, I'm No Businessperson, What Now?

I know, I know, you don't want to hear it again. You didn't want to hear it the first time either, but tough. Art is a business and as a working professional artist, you will be "in business" for yourself, just as much as a corner store owner, or the founder of a Fortune 500 company.

For some reason, when it comes to art, there's a reluctance to accept the commercial nature of the endeavor. Maybe it's something about the creative process, or the aesthetic nature of it that romanticizes it, sort of putting it above the crass bluntness of bean counting and schedules. That's all well and good, but romance and lofty notions about the noble nature of fine art won't feed you and it sure won't keep a roof over your head. The sooner you accept that being a working, selling artist is a business, your business, the better off you'll be. Luckily, you don't need an MBA to be successful. But you will need some discipline and some common sense.

I know you want to spend your days playing with paint and doing little else, but that's not practical, is it? And if you've gotten this far, you aren't doing that anyway. You're already running your business without even realizing it. You have your website, you post your work on social media, you share your blog, that's marketing. You answer emails and messages about your work, set prices and accept money. That's sales. You ship out paintings and provide tracking numbers to your collectors. That's customer service. And I would hope you're at least trying to keep track of what's coming in and what you're spending on supplies, shipping etc. Well, that's accounting. See? Business.

Of course, if you're anything like me, you either really dislike these tasks, or are woefully bad at some of them. No one is good at everything, that's why businesses hire people. An owner of a business assembles people with strengths he or she lacks that are necessary to the success of the operation. Well, I know you can't afford to pay anyone, but look around, you may have a perfect team already assembled.

Look at who you're sitting beside right now, your wife, partner, husband, or snuggle bunny. I'll bet they have skills you lack, or they like tasks you don't. Assuming they're supportive of your ambitions, they'd likely be more than happy to pitch in and give YOU Inc. a few hours a month. I got my wife involved with my art and she's been a great help. She's organized, detail oriented, and excels at keeping track of things, all things I am not. She's also extremely adept at handling me, calming me down, making sure I don't make too big a fool of myself. It was the best decision I ever made, and it frees me up with more time to do what I do best, paint, and doodle and paint some more.

Now that we've got your mindset right, we can jump into some of the finer aspects of the art business in the coming chapters. I'm not going to lie, it's a tough business, one of the toughest out there. The competition is stiff. The internet is full of people claiming to be artists, offering their work for sale. Sure, lots of it may not be nearly as good as what you're doing, but they're still out there, doing the same thing you are, showing their work, marketing themselves, competing for the same views, likes and collectors. And some of them will be way better than you are at those promotion and marketing tasks. As I think I've made clear, it takes time and a sustained and concerted effort to build an online presence and a reputation as a known artist.

Secondly, let's be brutally honest here, times are tough. People don't have the disposable income they had even a couple years ago. The pandemic and resulting recession have not only caused millions of people to lose their jobs but has also instilled a sense of fear for the future in many. Many have barely enough to cover the necessities of life, food, and shelter, and those that do have a little extra are inclined to hang onto it, just in case. When it comes to a beautiful painting or groceries, groceries win, hands down, every time.

However, it's not all doom and gloom. Tough times also bring opportunities. Remember the Great Depression? Well, I don't either, at least first hand, I wasn't born, but I have read a great deal about it and one fun fact that has stuck with me is that during that era, a time of great poverty and turmoil, lipstick sales

skyrocketed. Women were going nuts for it!
Seems odd, doesn't it? People are starving,
there's no work to be found and lipstick, of all
things, is flying off the shelves.

The thing is, it's not odd at all. Once
you think about it, it makes perfect sense. In
troubled times, people seek out comfort, small
luxuries to soothe them, to distract them from
the harsh realities of daily life, to make them
feel better, if only for a moment. It's simple
human nature. For Depression Era women, the
small luxury of being able to have brightly
coloured, pretty lips was a much-needed boost in
an otherwise dreary time.

I've sold several pieces during the
pandemic, throughout the shutdown, just when

things were at their scariest and most dire.
Why? Because art is like the lipstick I just
described. For those people fortunate enough to
be able to, it's a necessary distraction from the
chaos all around. You may have to be a bit
flexible in your pricing, but you can sell art even
in the worst of times.

The great thing about the art business is
that although it's tough, and although you're
going to work harder than you ever have in your
life, it's also the most rewarding business I can
think of being involved in. First, you get to
express yourself, to share bits of yourself with
others in a way that few others can ever do. You
know the old saying, a picture's worth a
thousand words, well a painting has to be worth
at least five thousand. In one painting, you can

express so many emotions, joy, pain, fear, and everything in between.

Better yet, you get to touch people's lives in ways others can't. A single painting can tell dozens of stories, evoke countless feelings or memories depending on who happens to be viewing it. Where one person sees a dark-haired girl on the beach, another sees the baby sister she lost 30 years ago, or the daughter she loves so much. And when your work touches someone in that special way, they'll share it with you, they'll open up to you, tell you about their lives, their feelings, their hopes and dreams. It's an instant deep, almost sacred connection with another human on this planet that you just don't get selling shoes or groceries.

Chapter 14: Paint What Sells or Sell What You

Paint

One of the most common questions
you'll see beginning artists asking is, "what
should I paint?" A variation on that theme is,
"what types of paintings sell the best?" You'll
find countless websites full of advice and lists of
the types of paintings that allegedly sell the best.
Those same sites will also advise you to paint
for the market; in other words, to paint the
subjects, in the colours that they say people
want. Sounds reasonable, right?

Wrong! These websites are so
completely off base that I can hardly figure out
where to begin. First, people are different, some

people like landscapes, others like animals, some like seascapes and others like portraits. There's a market for pretty much everything. The same goes for colours and styles.

Secondly, if I haven't made this clear already, artistic expression doesn't work that way. Artists are not machines that mass produce on demand. We're thinking, feeling human beings that pour our hearts and souls into our work, and if we do it correctly, the viewer can see it. It doesn't matter what the subject is, it could be a landscape of the ocean or a crow on an umbrella. It could be abstract. It could be pastel or brightly coloured. If the talent is there and you've created it from an honest place, it will find a home.

I mentioned several times, but it bears repeating here, art collectors are quite savvy, especially once they get to know your work. They can separate the wheat from the chaff. They know the pieces you created from pure artistic expression and emotion and the ones you threw together for quick sale. The latter have a flatness to them, a lack of emotion that is obvious.

The truth is, there is no type of painting that sells best. There is no one subject or colour or style that all people like best. Forget these websites and paint what you love to paint the way you love to paint it. Remember, you're trying to set yourself apart from the crowd, not be part of it.

Chapter 15: Name Your Price

Figuring out what to charge for your work is likely the hardest thing when you're starting out. There is a plethora of advice out there, just Google "how to price art" and you'll find pages and pages of so-called experts telling you how to do it. From price per square inch formulas to materials plus time calculations, they all sound logical enough and they're all essentially useless. That may sound harsh, and there are some good points sparsely scattered throughout some of these articles, but art pricing is both much simpler and much more complicated than that.

Let me illustrate with an example. Take two artists, A and B, both of equal talent and experience. Both decide to use the materials plus time pricing method. Both create equally beautiful pieces on 24 x 24" canvases. Both spend an equal amount on materials, we'll say $20. Both have decided that to make a living, they have to charge $20 an hour for their time. Artist A is a slow, methodical kind of cat, he takes his time, and his painting took 20 hours to complete. Artist B is a renegade, he gets hit by a lightning bolt of inspiration, slaps some paint around and in 2 hours creates a masterpiece. Following the time plus materials method A's painting is worth $420 and B's is worth $60. Hmmmmm.

Let's take this example even further. Now, let's assume there aren't two artists, there's just one, you. You've decided to use the same formula as artists A and B with the same cost for materials and the same $20 an hour for your time. You create 2 paintings, both 24 x 24" in a month. Both are exceptionally good, but one took you 5 hours because you were in the zone that day. The creative juices were flowing freely, and you were inspired beyond belief. It was as if the painting just "fell out of you". The second one, while just as beautiful, was harder going, the flow wasn't as easy, you found yourself having to go back to it over several days to get it "just right" and it took you 20 hours in total. You post both, but one is $120 and the other is $420 according to your pricing formula. Think about that for a minute. Put yourself in a collector's shoes. When you find out you paid $300 more for a painting of the same size than someone else who just paid $120, you're going to be livid! You, as a collector, will feel completely ripped off and rightfully so. The artist has just lost any credibility he had.

And if you think people don't talk, think again, word gets around. I once read a study that said that for every positive comment a person passes on about a business, they pass on 11 negative ones. The fact is, people just aren't going to fully understand or accept such a wide variation in price. There's no consistency, no predictability in it and people need that level of comfort and consistency to trust you enough to hand their money over to you. Think about it in simpler terms for a moment. On a much smaller scale, let's say there's a place you like to get coffee at. One day a large cup is $2.00, the next day it's $3.50, then it's back down to $2 and then up to $3, all for the same coffee of the same size. You won't be long finding a new place to get your morning caffeine infusion, right?

The reason there's no consistency in the materials plus costs method is because there's no consistency in artistic flow. Inspiration hits when it hits and some paintings, even of identical sizes, take longer than others. It can be for any number of reasons, mood, the number of distractions, the music you're playing, the weather. I've had paintings almost fall out of me, and I've had others I've agonized over for days. The flow is unpredictable, but you can't afford to be, at least as far as pricing goes.

Price per square inch has some appeal in that at least it's consistent, and I use a somewhat modified version of it. Price per square inch works like this, if you charge $1 per square inch, you multiply the length of the painting by the width and then multiply that by the $1. So, the price for a 24 x 24" piece would be:

24 x 24= 576 x $1 = $576

Obviously, starting out, you're not going to charge $1 per square inch for a piece. You know what you're going to charge? As silly as it sounds, you're going to charge what people are willing to pay combined with what you're willing to let the piece go for. I'm no economist, but I'm quite sure that's where supply meets demand. It takes some trial and error and a fair bit of research. Look around at other artists that are in a similar experience bracket as you, a similar number of shows, a similar number of years painting, check out their prices, most people post prices right on their site or on social media (I don't, more on that later). Convert that into a rough price per square inch. Starting out, keep yourself in a similar range as the contemporaries you've researched. You can make slight adjustments up or down depending on your sales. If you get no interest at a certain price point for a sustained period of time, adjust down a tick and conversely, if you're selling like hotcakes for a year straight, you may be able to nudge prices up a tick. Eventually, you get a feel for it.

Now, about posting prices. I mentioned that I don't. That goes against all the advice I've ever read, or at least most of it. Business experts love to expound about how you "have to make it easy" for today's consumer, how they're lazy. They want to click and collect. I've found the opposite to be the case. When someone is interested in a piece, they have no problem contacting me and asking the price and the size (although the size is always posted). More often than not, they want to chat a bit, to tell me about why they like the piece. I suspect they also want to size me up a bit, to get a feel for the man behind the paint. Am I trustworthy? Am I a snob? What was my inspiration for the piece?

Don't discount these conversations, they are more valuable than that one sale. I mentioned how great it is to touch people's lives before, but there's more to it than that. In those conversations, even if they don't buy right then, you've established a rapport, you'll both walk away from the exchange with a positive experience. They'll be back, when finances improve, when another piece touches them in a way they can't resist. They'll tell their friends. And, if they do buy, they become a valued collector and may well be back for more. Most of my collectors have an average of 3 pieces, and most have introduced their friends and family to my work. Word of mouth is a wonderful thing, and people buy from people they like, not people they don't like.

I also prefer a conversation regarding price over a listed price for another reason. I offer a payment plan. Yeah, you heard me, a payment plan. You won't need this right away, but as your work increases in value, you may.

The simple fact is, you're selling a luxury good and sometimes, you must meet people where they're at. There are many, many people out there that may want to collect your art, but they just don't have several hundreds of dollars to plop down in one shot. People have circumstances, bills, kids in college, mortgage payments, car payments, life stuff. I'm willing to work with these people and you should be too, their money is as green as anyone else's.

My payment plan works as follows; I charge a non-refundable deposit up front. That's to secure the piece and to compensate me for no longer offering it for sale. The deposit can be any amount you want, but it must be both reasonable and enough that the buyer won't want to forfeit it. And the deposit is due immediately. Then, after a conversation with the buyer, you determine both the timing and the amount of future payments. Some people are paid weekly, others every 2 weeks and some once a month. Be very clear on the terms and be sure you keep track of the payments accurately. Most people are surprisingly good about making their payments on time and as agreed. Some need gentle reminders, and you can do this tactfully and gracefully. I've sold countless pieces this way and I could never have done that

without having a conversation about price.

Bottom line invite people to approach you,

you'll be glad you did.

Chapter 16: People to Avoid 1: You're Simply Irresistible Now

Now that I've got your attention, I do realize I have no idea what you look like. And you know what? It doesn't matter because even if you're a very overweight middle-aged man with thinning hair, you're about to become a whole lot sexier to a whole lot of people. And you'll do it without the aid of diet, exercise, or Botox treatments. Just the simple fact that you're an artist, for some reason, as you become better and better known, seems to make you irresistible to some member of the opposite, and the same sex.

It's a strange phenomenon, but for some reason, there's a subset of the population that is fascinated by artists! Maybe it's the romantic notion of the starving, brooding, incredibly handsome young artist that takes the middle-aged bored and frustrated housewife to his loft studio and gets creative with her in more ways than one. Maybe it's the idea that us artistic types are somehow more sensitive than others. I honestly have no idea and I've spent more time than any human should on thinking about it, to no avail. I don't know why it's so; I just know it is.

If you're anything like I was, a fat 40 - something man with thinning hair, the newfound attention can be exciting. Suddenly, people want to talk to you, they get crushes on you, they just want to be part of your orbit in some way. And if you're anything like me, you'll fall into the age-old trap of thinking sex sells, it sells everything from whiskey to cars, so why not art? What could it hurt to let Joe or Jane have their little fantasy about you as long as they're buying your work?

Quite a bit of harm, as it turns out. First, leading people on, for any reason is just a jerk move. Second, it's not worth the hassle. I can hear you arguing with me. You're thinking, hey it's money, a few hundred bucks is worth a bit of time spent making someone feel wanted. But here's the thing, most of these people who develop a fixation on you will be, well, I want to be nice, so let's just say, many will struggle with reality. Hopefully you'll see sense once I tell you some of the missteps I've made in this department. Before I do, I do want to preface these anecdotes by saying I wasn't initially aware that the individuals in question had a thing for me. I'm woefully blind about such things, but it did eventually become evident and in many instances, by that time, it also became too late to extricate myself gracefully and without hurt feelings.

First up there was a woman in California, we'll call her Lisa. This was in the early stages of my online art career. She saw my work and soon became one of my biggest fans. She ordered several paintings totalling some four figures and asked if she could send a money order for the price. I agreed and promptly shipped the pieces (note, never ever ship your art to a collector until you've received the purchase price in full and have transferred it to your bank). She somehow managed to convince me to take our online chats to telephone calls and began throwing around the idea of me moving to the US with her. She even paid for a psychic to call me to "tell me about my future". All the while she was well aware of my then live-in girlfriend. Eventually, I got the idea that she fancied me, and I decided it would be best, both for my relationship at the time and for Lisa, to cool things off. Not ghost her or anything like that, just to be less available every time she wanted a chat. A gentle nudge to let her know I had other things going on in my life.

Lisa didn't like that. She didn't like that one bit. She cancelled the money order. Having already shipped the paintings, I obviously wanted my money, so I dove back in, being super available to her whenever she wanted. So here I was, tied to the computer or the phone, for hours on end, with a woman I didn't know, didn't like in any romantic way and had never even seen a picture of. She, of course, immediately reinstated the money order. I backed off a bit, she cancelled again. Each and every time she felt she wasn't getting the attention from me she felt she was due, she stopped payment. Finally, I played nice, gave her all the attention she wanted, waited for the money order to arrive and clear, and deleted and blocked her. I'm sure her feelings were hurt and I'm sure she told all her friends what a horrible person I was. Bad news travels a lot faster than good.

Along the same lines, there was Betsy, an older lady, in her 60's, I think. I met Betsy through her daughter and Betsy soon became a fan and began collecting my work. She wasn't able to buy them outright, so she always made payments. And the payments were always a struggle to get. She would talk to me for hours, demanding increasing amounts of my time and throwing tantrums when I couldn't talk to her. She failed or refused to make scheduled payments as agreed. She would only pay if I was online and willing to talk with her. Getting a $50 payment often cost me 4 hours of my evening, and that was when she wasn't in a chatty mood. That's four hours I could have spent working, or with my wife. Again, I had to delete and block her, which led to a barrage of online abuse on other channels, including my wife's Facebook page. More hurt feelings, more bashing and badmouthing.

Not all of these, we'll call them "love collectors" are not quite so petulant about things. Some are much more subtle and clever, but the result is always the same. Case in point, Alice, a surgical nurse from Texas or somewhere started collecting my work. She was married, so I figured there'd be no issue. Things started out great, she bought a few of my paintings, and we'd chat a bit, about mundane things, life, work, the weather. Somehow, over the course of a few weeks, she was ordering paintings hand over fist, but rather than getting them outright, she'd ask me to hold them, till her next pay. I figured why not, she was good for the money, having already paid for a handful of pieces. She began messaging me constantly, upon waking, throughout her workday, the evening on and on. My wife warned me she was getting too attached, but I didn't listen. When her payday came and went, I asked her about the pieces she had asked me to set aside. That's when the excuses started, the car broke down, there was an emergency, whatever. She continued to consume more and more of my time until I was literally on the computer with her 6 or 7 hours a day, much to the dismay of my wife. Another two weeks, another pay cycle and I asked again. She didn't respond and a few weeks later I got an angry message from her about what a jerk I was, and she blocked me. The "Alice" type situation happens quite a lot so watch out for it.

There was also the gay guy from Denmark who took a shine to me, began eating up all my time and every time I pulled back, he threatened to harm himself. Scary stuff. He eventually got the hint because I began continually injecting little anecdotes about my wife into our conversations. He didn't like that.

No amount of money is worth the hurt these situations cause both to the person who has the crush and potentially to your reputation and your current relationship if you're in one. But how can you tell if a person is a true fan and collector or someone out for more than you're willing to give?

It's not easy to tell sometimes, not for me at least. My wife seems to be able to spot them a mile away. My advice would be as follows:

1. Keep the conversations professional yet pleasant;

2. Don't allow yourself to get tied into conversations too long, if things seem to be taking a strange or more personal tone than you're comfortable with, cut it short, say you have to run, get back to work, go to an appointment, anything;

3. Don't allow anyone to make purchase or payment contingent upon you're being there to chat. Anyone who is serious about collecting your work will not need you to hold their hand while they use

PayPal or whatever payment processing system you use;

4. If you're in a relationship, gently slide that fact into conversations by mentioning your significant other (things like, "yeah, my wife/husband loves poetry too" or "I was just talking to my wife/husband about the same thing") and do it often, or post some cute pics of you and them together on your feed.

These steps will generally help you separate the wheat from the chaff, as it were. Most people with romantic notions will eventually get the hint and leave of their own accord, as long as you don't entertain them, leaving the serious fans and collectors with you to continue to love

and buy your work.

Chapter 17: People to Avoid 2: the "Unofficial Manager"

As you can see, I could write an entire book on the types of people to avoid as an aspiring professional artist and near, the top of the list is the" unofficial manager". This is the person, who, well meaning or not, has taken it upon themselves to take charge of all things relating to you and your work. Their motivations can range from a sincere desire to help to a longing to be "in the art world" with all it's glamour, or to elevate their social status by positioning themselves as having "discovered" you. Whatever their motivation, they want a piece of your pie without having been offered any at all. When you see these people coming, you can decide just how fast you need to walk or run in the other direction. Just how fast you move will be in direct proportion to just how pushy they are.

The "unofficial manager" shows up in a variety of places, online, among your family, sometimes even in your own home and the closer they are to you, the harder they can be to manage.

For example, many years ago, when my sales through social media really took off, I was living with a woman who took it upon herself to help me on my art path. She fancied herself some sort of an expert and began policing, to some extent what I painted. If I went outside the box, was a bit experimental, did something other than what had already been proven to be the subject and style of a "quick seller", she'd quickly dismiss the piece as not up to scratch. She was quite an argumentative and disagreeable woman in the first place, so I often acquiesced to her assessments.

The problem is, expression, particularly artistic expression must be able to grow. Experimenting with new styles, new subjects and new pallets is essential to the growth and development of an artist. When you're a kid and you learn to read, you don't stick with Dick and Jane forever, you try harder and harder books, with bigger words and less pictures until you're reading War and Peace. You exercise that muscle, so it grows, develops, and improves. Creating is no different. How on earth will you find your own style without trying a few out? When you stifle an artist, you'll get stifled and stagnated work, not to mention a very unhappy artist. Did I mention I left that particular woman?

Now don't get me wrong. I'm not saying to close yourself off from constructive criticism. There will be times that someone has made a valid point and there's no shame in taking that on board. But there's a difference between constructive criticism and outright dismissal of any deviation for a so-called norm.

Some experiments work out and others don't, just like any other learning and growing process, but I can say I've learned from all of them. And some of my very best, most memorable pieces have been the result of being able to throw off the shackles of what's been done, what can be done, what should be done and just let the paint fly. In fact, one very early experiment was my first significant sale at a show. I painted a piece called Old City, it had many more abstract elements to it than my earlier work and something about it was just amazingly compelling. I put it in a show for emerging artists in Toronto (this was back in the days before social distancing when there were still art shows), and it sold for $500 before the show had even formally opened to the public. A wealthy gentleman from the US who happened to be vacationing popped in and saw it and his wife HAD to have it! To this day, that painting, and its sale is one of the highlights of my career.

Over the years since then, I've experimented some more, and often abstract elements will show up in my work which has created my signature style. It's very easy to identify one of my pieces by this style.

The takeaway here is simple, don't let anyone fence you in. Don't let them define you or your work. Allow yourself the room to experiment and learn and grown. You may have to get firm, but so be it, this is your career we're talking about.

Another variation of the unofficial manager is the fan turned manager. This is the person who has collected your work, but for some reason or another, has decided to elevate themselves from collector to an integral part of the organization (p.s.: everybody knows the collector is the most integral part of the organization.). They're often among the most persistent, let's be honest, downright pushy, because having bought your work, they feel somehow entitled to have a stake in your career. These are often people, who although maybe meaning well, are afflicted with a very fragile ego and a strong need to appear to belong to a higher social status than their peers. Because of this, they can be particularly difficult to manage.

I've had several "fans turned managers" over the years and the relationship never ends well. I'll give you an example.

There was a woman from the Southwestern U.S., we'll call her Arlene, she found me on social media and became a fan and a collector. We chatted some, and I knew she was a bit of a pretentious sort, but whatever, I'm not here to judge, everyone's money is good with me. Over the course of a few weeks, the suggestions started, "you should try using more of a Midwest colour scheme", "you should teach my daughter", "you should come out here and I'll take you around", "you should change this or that on your website", you get the idea. She began becoming quite insistent to the point where she continually interjected herself into every post I made and any ensuing replies to said posts. And I do mean Every. Single. Post. And these weren't short, friendly replies like, "yes, Jenny, it is a beautiful piece, isn't it?" or "I like it too". The replies, and there were always several for each post, were long, drawn out soliloquies all about her, using my work as the background, and having very little, if anything to do with the actual post, except maybe an admonishment to buy a piece, things like:

> *"As a person who has several of his paintings, I never ever quibble on price. I always pay what the artist asks because I support the arts, I am a patron of the arts one might say. If you don't know what a patron is it's someone who supports the arts. I do that because I am a person of good breeding and education, having been educated both overseas and at Harvard. I have many degrees, but I am not a snob. I am a*

good person. You should be a good

person too and do yourself a favour and

buy one of his pieces."

Or

"As a person owning X number of

Carl's pieces, and a multi-degreed

professional, I have remodeled my

extremely large country home to

accommodate his work. Even my

daughter, who is also an extremely

talented artist, in her own right, is

impressed by his work. I never even ask

the price, I just pay what he wants and

as a person of faith, I believe art is

essential. If you haven't gotten one of

his paintings yet, I'm not sure what it is

you're waiting for."

This kind of "help" is not the kind of
help any artist needs. As you can see, it smacks
of haughty arrogance and is frankly insulting
and demeaning to anyone who reads it. I knew I
had to gently tell this woman that while I
appreciated the sentiment, her posts were off-
putting to some (pretty much everyone). I
didn't. I was a coward, plain and simple.

Things escalated to her not only
continuing to post, but also continually bringing
her suggestions to me and offers of help, again
all unsolicited. She'd redo my website, she'd
rewrite my bio, she'd write a glowing
testimonial. She was soon taking up hours of

my time with her plans for me and my art. At this point, even my wife, who is my actual official manager, was beyond annoyed and she offered me an ultimatum, get this woman in line nicely, or she'd do it, not quite as nicely. Being the coward that I was, I hid behind my wife/manager, and told Arlene that anything she wanted to write would have to be given to my wife for review. Funny, the "glowing" posts, the unsolicited ideas and offers of her self-styled "expertly written content" dried up almost immediately.

Do I feel bad about hiding behind my wife? Yes and no. No because as my manager, dealing with people and protecting me is her job. Yes, because, I deliberately stuck my head in the sand to avoid confrontation. Maybe I was hoping to sell her more paintings, or maybe I didn't want to hurt her feelings, but whatever it was, just like the countless times similar things have happened before Arlene and after, I let it go too far, so far there was no graceful way out.

What I learned from all this, and it took me a few tries to get the lesson, is that as a person in business for yourself, you've got to get yourself a backbone. You have to learn where your professional boundaries are and draw that line in a clear, bright red marker. You must learn to say no when no is the answer. You can say it nicely, but you have to say it. Something simple like, "thank you, but I have someone that handles those things," usually works, it's simple, to the point, and polite.

The unofficial manager can be one of the most detrimental influences on an artist. Our innate desire to please and our eagerness to expand our fan base and sales leaves us vulnerable to unsolicited advice that might, on the surface, appear reasonable. Just like too many cooks spoil the broth, too many managers spoil the art.

Chapter 18: People to Avoid 3: A Short
Note on "Exposure"

Another type of person you'll encounter
on your journey, and another you'll wish to
avoid is the person who offers exposure in
exchange for a free piece of art. Honestly, this
is the type of person I find most annoying and
sadly, you will encounter a lot of them!

The offer of exposure for a freebie is as
old as time itself. It happens in almost any
creative context you can think of. "Hey man, I
love your band, why don't you come play at my
wedding. I can't pay you, but the exposure
would be great," or "your books are awesome, I
wish I could afford to buy them, but if you give

me free copies, I'll promote you all over." You get the idea.

Frankly, the offer of exposure in lieu of purchase price is downright insulting. You can't eat it. You can't pay your bills with it. When was the last time you called the power company and offered them exposure, so they'd keep your lights on? The fact is, these people are seeking to take advantage of you, to use your excitement and desire to gain a larger following, to get free things for themselves.

Follow my logic for a minute and you'll see I'm right. More often than not, these people will begin their pitch with a declaration of poverty. They have no money, they can't afford your work, they have circumstances, you see.

Hold that thought in your mind while we continue breaking down their pitch. Next, they'll present the offer of "exposure" and all they want is a free piece. Then they'll wax eloquently about all they can do for you. They know everybody who is anybody, all the movers and shakers, all the important people, monied people. They're brilliant in using social media and are super adept at digital marketing, heck, they're practically an influencer. They can write better than Shakespeare and can write poems to accompany your art that will make even the hardest heart cry. Their credentials are impressive, so impressive you begin to seriously think about their offer. Again, I'll give you a real-life example from the Big Book of Carl.

Velma was a woman who enjoyed my work. She always complained about being broke, and I knew she was telling the truth. She wanted to have my paintings but couldn't afford them and was upfront about that fact. However, she had an idea. She even came to my home, driving over an hour, twice, to discuss it.

She came in, sat down, and boy, to hear her talk, you'd believe she just came from lunch with the Queen herself! She could get me in with all the right people, her personal friends, all doctors, "John, and Don." She had studied post-impressionist art at the Metropolitan Museum of Art in New York and therefore was somewhat of an expert. She knew all the businesspeople in the area and dropped their names. She was brilliant at social media; she was a mover and a shaker of the highest order. I had to admit, I was impressed, because I was blinded by the possibilities (false as they were). She even had that "air" about her, like she could walk the walk as well as talk the talk. She was even haughtily dismissive of my wife, as if our conversation had nothing to do with her and she should run along and let the grown folks talk business. Big mistake.

I almost agreed to hand over two paintings that Velma had picked out for herself then and there. That's when my wife stepped in, pulled me aside and suggested I give the matter some thought. I agreed and boy am I glad I did.

Sometimes we artistic types live with our heads in the clouds. It may sound awful, but it's true. We take people at their word, we're

dreamers. Our heads are filled with beauty and

paint, there's not a lot of room for common

sense. With that in mind, I'm going to give you

the gift of just that, common sense, hopefully

it'll save you the trouble I've had.

We'll take dear Velma as an example.

First her credentials. She knew the first names

of her doctors. Great, I also know the first name

of my doctor, my dentist, and the President of

the United States, it doesn't mean I have any

sort of personal relationship with any of them.

Same thing with the assorted names of members

of the local business community she dropped. I

know the first names of the guy who runs the

corner store, the woman who runs that Italian

restaurant I like and the founder of Microsoft. I don't know any of them personally.

She claimed to have studied at the Metropolitan Museum of Art in New York. The Met is just that, a museum, not a university. They do offer workshops, tours, and things like that, and I'm sure they're excellent and very educational. I'd love to someday visit myself and take advantage. However, taking a museum tour and talk in an afternoon is hardly "studying post-impressionist art," now is it?

She also claimed to be a social media guru. I checked her social media. I'm not sure 12 Instagram followers constitute guru status.

Then there are the cries of poverty. This is the one you'll really find both funny and infuriating at the same time. And it's the one

that shows all the other claims for what they are,

complete and utter bull! First, you've heard the

saying, "birds of a feather flock together." Have

you ever considered what it means? If not, think

about it now. It means people tend to seek out

and hang out with those that are like them,

similar interests, similar economic brackets.

When's the last time you heard of a doctor or a

lawyer hanging socially with someone on the

skids? Do you think the Queen is inviting the

local garbage man over for tea and crumpets? Of

course not!

Secondly, if a person is all that they say

they are; if they are so adept at promoting

others, at doing this and that, why are they so

broke? Why aren't they promoting themselves

and whatever it is they're good at? Oh, wait, I know, because what they're good at is conning others into thinking they're good at something so they can get free stuff! Not this guy, and now, not you either!

Chapter 19: A Brief Note on Card Tricks

Although much of the world is online, you'll still meet people out and about in the physical world. And when businesspeople meet, what do they do? They exchange contact details, and they do this via the age-old staple, the business card. They're inexpensive, you can get 500 of them for less than $20 and they contain all the information relevant to contacting you, your name, your website, and email. You can put your address and phone number on there too if you want. I don't put my phone number on mine as it's my personal preference to keep a tight reign on my private life and space.

Get yourself some business cards, place a few in your wallet or purse and when meeting people, pass one along. There's nothing worse than posing as a professional and when asked for your contact information, you have nothing to offer. Having them at the ready gives you that credibility. And you never know when someone may look at it, check out your website and find something they like, maybe even like enough to buy.

To be perfectly honest, I take the business card even further than this. Maybe it's sneaky, maybe it's just plain brilliant, I don't know, I do it anyway. When I'm out and about, stopping for coffee, having dinner out, at the airport waiting on a flight, I'll discreetly leave one of my cards on the seat or the table, a kind of "Carl wuz here." The card itself only costs a couple cents and you never know who might pick it up, look at it and check out your work.

I have no way of knowing how many sales I've received as a result of my "card trick," no one has ever come up to me and said, "hey, I found your business card and decided to buy a painting." Then again, no one has told me they found my card and didn't.

Chapter 20: Stop Working and Join the World

After chapter after chapter of telling you how hard this was going to be and how you're going to have to work your guts out, I'm going to tell you to stop working for a while. I can see you shaking your head. Look, I'm not telling you to quit. I'm telling you to work hard, but also play hard, love hard, smell the roses.

There's more to life than art. I know it's hard to realize that when you're in the throws of trying to build a career. It's especially hard when you begin to sell and feel the irresistible thrill of each sale. It's intoxicating! The thing is, you gotta feed the machine.

Cars need gas and oil and regular maintenance and if they go too long without those things, they just stop running one day. You're no different, and neither was I.

First, take time to maintain your health. Eat your meals, proper meals, actual food. Walk away from the easel and sit down at the dining room table and eat. I avoided doing this for years, opting to paint and eat hot dogs or maybe a quick bowl of some boxed noodle concoction. I ended up topping the scales at close to 400 pounds. I was fat, I was tired, but I was painting. God knows how long I could have kept it up; it scares me to think about it now. The funny thing about abusing your body is you can do it for quite some time, you begin to forget what healthy feels like and being sluggish and sickly becomes the new normal. You can keep rolling on like that, until one day, you can't, because you're dead or you've given yourself a stroke or a heart attack.

Get some exercise. Go outside. You remember outside, right, it's that place right outside your front door, there's air and trees and grass and all kinds of nature stuff. A lot of the stuff out there might be things you like to paint. Don't you think maybe you should look at them for real? Go for a walk. Take your camera. Take pictures of cool things you see that inspire you. You can't get inspired by staring at the same 4 walls day in and day out.

Remember the things you loved to do before you embarked on this journey and make time to do them. Ride a bike, go swimming, sing silly songs, continue those Kung Fu lessons, whatever it is, do it. In order to work effectively, you have to walk away from the work to renew yourself. Why do you think people get vacation time? You have to have vacation time.

Speaking of vacations, go on one every now and again. See that country you always wanted to see. Go see the ocean or the icebergs or New York City. Heck, go camping 5 miles down the road, go for a drive, just go somewhere and do anything but paint, think of paint or related to paint. You'll come back bursting with ideas, inspiration, and energy!

And while you're at it, remember to join the human race, especially at home. Make your partner happy, they're in this with you. Take some time for them. Sit, talk, hang out, play a board game, have a romantic evening. And if you want that romantic evening, do something drastic, do the dishes, take out the trash, maybe make supper. The world, and the household chores don't stop just because you've decided you're an artist now. Trust me, you'll get much more cooperation when you need to devote your undivided attention to art stuff if you've chipped in with the chores regularly. No one wants to live with a demanding diva who is entirely too important for the mundane household tasks. You eat, you make garbage and you dirty dishes, take some responsibility for yourself and your home. You'll be glad you did.

A one-dimensional person will be a one-dimensional artist, boring, stale, and tired. Step away from the art so you can step back in better than ever. In fact, you won't just be a better artist, you'll be a better person.

www.ingramcontent.com/pod-product-compliance
Lightning Source LLC
Chambersburg PA
CBHW070547220526
45467CB00003B/1113